Northumberland's Lost Houses

A picture postcard history by Jim Davidson

Edited by Hilary Kristensen

Northumberland's Lost Houses

Jim Dixon.
12.08.

Contents

Foreword by Viscount Allendale

"I feel very honoured to have been asked to write a foreword to Jim Davidson's book **'Northumberland's Lost Houses'**. While it is sad that we have lost so many fantastic and varied buildings, it is wonderful that Jim has devoted so much time and effort into producing such a worthwhile record.

This book will appeal to many people and I hope it will serve to remind us all that we really cannot afford to lose any more of these fascinating examples of our heritage."

The Viscount Allendale
Bywell Castle
November 2008

Introduction

Country house building in Northumberland followed a different pattern of development to that found in other English counties. Until the union between England and Scotland in 1603, anyone wealthy enough to contemplate the building of a large house had to think about warlike incursions from Scotland. Indeed many border families ignored the border line altogether and feuding took place between various *graynes* (men sharing a family name), the Northumbrian equivalent of the Scottish clan system. With this threat possible from either side of the disputed border, anyone building anything more than the most basic dwelling had to consider some form of fortification. This ranged from the simplest fortified bastle house to the grandest of castles. The great nobles built their castles and the humble farmers their bastles, but the gentry equivalent of the country houses which had already appeared in the rest of England took the form of fortified towers in Northumberland.

These towers varied greatly in both size and style. The simplest was the pele tower and these sprang up all over the county. The example shown (left) is the fourteenth century **Vicars Pele** at Ponteland, now an empty shell. These houses were mainly occupied by the minor gentry or, as in this case, the clergy.

The grander gentry had correspondingly larger dwellings. The tower house was a more substantial version of the pele tower, and fifteenth century **Cocklaw Tower** near Chollerton (below) is a fine example.

Vicars Pele, Ponteland.

Cocklaw Tower, Chollerton

The strong house was the next stage of development. A rectangular rather than square floor plan, larger windows, a staircase tower and pitched roof, formed a building that was much closer to our modern day view of what a house should look like. **Doddington**, built in 1584, and shown here (right) in a picture of 1880 is a prime example. It is now a ruin (below right) but its fine staircase tower still stands proud.

Cartington Castle.

Fortified manor houses formed the last stage in development before the arrival of the country house proper. **Cartington Castle** started life as a pele tower but was added to and altered over the centuries into the house we see (above). It had become so ruinous that Lord Armstrong directed and paid for stabilising work which was carried out in the 1880s, shortly after which this view was taken.

The union of 1603 saw little change in house building in Northumberland. The county was comparatively poor and many of the local gentry lacked the confidence and wealth to embark on ambitious new house building projects. Many satisfied their limited ambitions by simply adding to their existing towers, **Belsay** (overleaf) being a typical example. The original fourteenth century tower house was extended in 1614 and again in 1711. These additions were completely

Doddington, complete in 1880 (above) and in ruins (left).

Belsay Castle.

Other unfortified houses began slowly to appear in Northumberland. Anderson Place had been built in 1580, but noticeably safely inside Newcastle's strong City Walls. Stotes Hall of 1607, and **Denton Hall** (below left) of 1622, however, were built well outside the protection of those same walls.

As the seventeenth century progressed, so the pace of country house building increased. The second half of the century was dominated by Robert Trollope of York, [? - 1686]. He was the first country house architect of Northumberland, building amongst others, Bockenfield in 1660, **Capheaton Hall** (below) in 1668 and Netherwitton Hall in 1685. Newcastle Guild Hall is perhaps his best known work but is very different now to Trollope's original design.

Capheaton Hall.

unfortified and the decoration and style used show a growing confidence and ambition in country house building. The tower house and extension of 1614 shown in the view (above) still survive. The further grand extension of 1711 only survived until the family moved from the Castle to the newly built Belsay Hall in 1817.

Denton Hall.

The arrival of the eighteenth century saw increased prosperity from booming agriculture and early industry that was reflected in a further increase in country house building. The local gentry now felt confident in building their houses further away from the major centres of population. The newly emerging professional and industrial middle classes however preferred to stay close to the larger towns, most noticeably Newcastle and Hexham. The landed classes built in the countryside and the newly rich just outside the towns. Benwell and Elswick were particularly favoured by this latter

Highgreen Manor.

the start. Many country houses have had large Victorian extensions removed leaving a smaller and more manageable house. Blagdon in Northumberland is a good example, losing some additions after severe fire damage in 1945.

Fortunately most built on a more practical scale. Isolated **Highgreen Manor** near Gatehouse was built in 1885 and is shown (left) after the completion of the extension of 1894.

Ramshawe in Corbridge was built in 1905 as a message from the owner, Mr A Dixon, tells us on the reverse of this postcard view (below). His message continues:

"The men have had this view taken for themselves. Hope to get in soon."

Ramshawe, Corbridge.

group and a contemporary description of these areas as a 'rural arcadia' seems somewhat fanciful today.

The eighteenth century equivalent of Robert Trollope in Northumberland was William Newton (1730-1798). He was followed in the nineteenth century by John Dobson (1787-1865). These two local architects designed or altered a huge proportion of the county's large houses. Although some nationally important architects designed houses in Northumberland, in particular James Paine (1716-1789), the importance of Trollope, Newton and Dobson cannot be overstated. To have them designing country houses in three succeeding centuries in one county is probably unique in English architectural history.

As elsewhere in the country, increased wealth and a plentiful labour supply saw country house development reach an extreme. The huge and never to be completed Twizell Castle was an early example in the county but in general it was the Victorians who built to such excess. The one hundred and fifty four roomed Haggerston Castle proved totally impracticable and these huge white elephants were perhaps doomed from

These pre-war views show us how plentiful and cheap building labour was still readily available, and also the labour intensive nature of the work prior to the arrival of mechanical diggers, cement mixers and the like. The pride that the men took in their work is also clearly evident.

Northumberland's country house development had finally caught up with the other English counties. Unfortunately, after the great late nineteenth and early twentieth century zenith of country house living, the county's losses were to prove equally numerous and tragic to the rest of the country.

The 1950s and 1960s were the two worst decades for country house losses in England. 1968 saw more country houses demolished than in any other year. Cynics might link this to the introduction of formal listed building consent from 1st January 1969. From this date, owners were legally obliged to seek permission to demolish and it would seem that many owners rushed to beat this deadline.

Reasons for the loss of so many country houses were many and varied. Prior to the First World War, the major culprit was fire. Large numbers of coal fires were needed to heat these huge houses. Many Northumberland country house owners had interests in the coal industry and consequently had large and cheap supplies of coal. Fires blazed merrily in the large family rooms and in the smaller servants' rooms, servants' hall and kitchen, an accident waiting to happen. Many of these houses were the first to be lit by gas and consequently had very basic gas supplies and appliances. Many country house owners still used large numbers of candles. They were also the earliest houses to be lit by electricity and early wiring was notoriously dangerous. The great risk of fire prompted many country house owners to establish their own miniature fire fighting units. Fire services tended to be centred in towns and a response to a fire in an isolated country house was necessarily slow. The view below shows **Fenham Hall**, now restored, after the fire of February 1908.

The fire at Fenham Hall.

The twentieth century growth of industry and rise in population was another factor in the demise of the country house, particularly those closer to large towns. Those areas of Benwell and Elswick so favoured by the newly rich nineteenth century industrialists for their country estates in miniature now proved to be not so desirable. Ironically, those industries that had made their owners wealthy were directly to blame. The large number of workers needed to service these industries needed somewhere to live. Terraced houses, chapels, churches and schools began to encroach on the once 'rural arcadia'. Fumes from chemical works, noise from shipyards, smells from leather works and unsightly gas works dramatically changed the green and pleasant land. The factory workers had to put up with it but the wealthy large house owners could leave it all behind. Those from Benwell and Elswick generally moved westward up the Tyne Valley and began a new country house enclave centred on the Hexham area rather than Newcastle. Better transport links and improved services made this less problematical and once again created a distance between the wealthy and their work force. Many of the large houses survived the loss of their owners and their parkland and were put into alternative use. Elswick Hall became a museum, **Benwell House** (right) an hotel, and Benwell Cottage a young men's hostel, before all finally disappearing in the 1970s. Some few still survive in alternative use today such as Benwell Tower, Pendower and the Dene.

The two Great Wars also played their part in the loss of many country houses. Some became army hospitals, company headquarters, and others were used for classified War work. The subsequent damage and spoliation caused to both houses, gardens and parkland by this occupation often proved to be irreversible. The compensation offered to the owners at the end of the War was often derisible and the future of the houses concerned bleak. The view (right) shows the ballroom at **Howick Hall** in use as an army hospital.

Benwell House.

Howick Hall.

Belford Hall.

Another nail in the coffin was the loss of a generation of country house heirs. Sons of the country house owners often entered the Services as junior officers expected to lead from the front. Being first out of the trenches, their death rate was disproportionately high and could lead to a situation of multiple inheritances. One young surviving heir could find himself with three inherited estates, all with large houses and impossible to run. Low land rents, a workforce who no longer wished to return to a life of service, and staggeringly high death duties, were for many old families, the death knell for life as they had known it. A small villa in Southern France or Northern Italy suddenly seemed a very desirable alternative to a life of servitude to a white elephant of a great house which had become a financially bottomless pit.

Fortunately, the tide turned. An increase in prosperity which began in the 1960s saw a rapid decline in country house losses in the 1970s, and this trend has continued until today. A new generation of pop stars, company directors and city high flyers discovered the joy of country house living. Many were restored to family use and those deemed too large for single family occupancy found a new role as luxury apartments. All the benefits of country house living but with all the upkeep and expenditure shared between fellow residents, as at **Belford Hall**, (above) converted in the 1980s.

Other houses were restored as company headquarters or as centres for various organisations, a clearly visible outward sign of their success.

The following pages are a record of those many Northumberland houses which didn't survive.

Gazetteer of Lost Houses

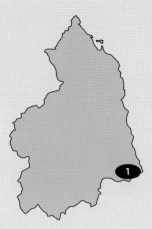

Anderson Place

NEWCASTLE – GREY STREET. *1580. Wings added 1675 - 1834.*

Called 'Newe House' when built in 1580 on the site now occupied by Grey Street, Anderson Place was the largest house ever built inside Newcastle's City Walls.

In Welford's 'Men of Mark', we learn that:

"In the spring of 1834, Mr Grainger purchased for £50,000 from Major George Anderson the fine old mansion and grounds called Anderson Place."

We can see from the plan above why this purchase was to be the starting point of Dobson and Grainger's re-development of central Newcastle.

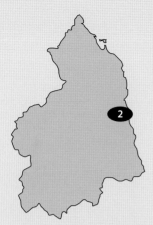

Bank House

ACKLINGTON. *Mid-1700s, enlarged 1799 - 1957.*

Its architectural similarities to other Northumberland country houses, particularly Close House and Togston Hall, suggests that Bank House was designed by William Newton. He was better known for re-fronting older houses and an earlier Bank House is known to have existed in the mid 1700s. Newton's best known surviving building is the Newcastle Assembly Rooms.

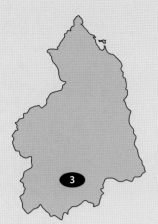

Beacon Grange

HEXHAM. *c.1700 - 1937.*

Situated to the south of Hexham between the surviving estates of Ochrelands and Loughbrow House, its grounds now form part of an enlarged Ochrelands estate. Nothing remains of Beacon Grange or its many outbuildings, walled garden, orchard and park all shown so clearly on the 1865 Ordnance Survey Map.

Beaconsfield House

CULLERCOATS. *1872 - 1959.*

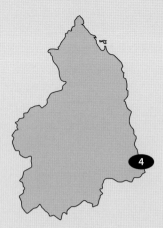

4

4

Built in 1872 by the philanthropist John Henry Burn for the enormous sum of £35,000, poor Beaconsfield House sold for only £5,000 in 1922 on the death of his widow. After use as a Barnardo's Home and then as a council run convalescent home, it was demolished in 1959. Burn generously gave the sites for several parish churches and vicarages in the suburbs of Newcastle. The Burn family still live in Northumberland at Carrycoats Hall.

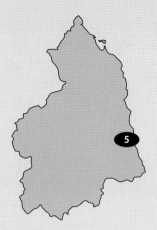

Bedlington Old Hall

BEDLINGTON. *c.1400s. Rebuilt and enlarged 1700s - 1958.*

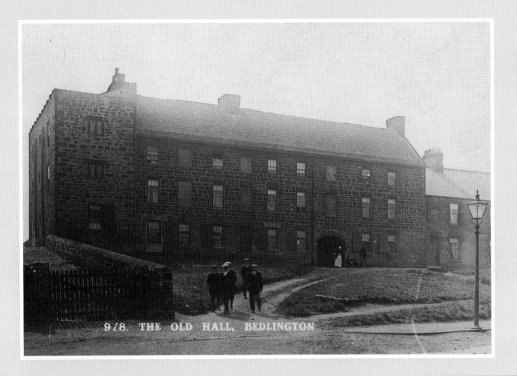

978. THE OLD HALL, BEDLINGTON

A fifteenth century pele tower with early eighteenth century additions, poor Bedlington Old Hall ended its life as a tenement block. Its sorry demolition was explained away thus by a local councillor:

"We propose to demolish the Old Hall and Keep which for centuries have dominated our Front Street. We desire to use that very desirable site in a much better way."

So much for progress!

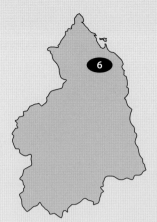

Bellshill

ADDERSTONE. *c.1780 - c.1947.*

Bellshill House.

The Bellshill estate was formed in 1780 by the purchase of eight hundred acres of land from the Adderstone estate by John Pratt, the buyer and builder of Bellshill. The house survived until 1947 but much of the estate had previously been sold off to neighbouring landowners and farmers.

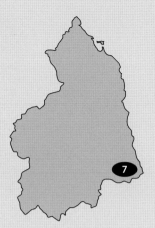

Benton Hall

BENTON. *1760 - c.1950.*

The Benton Hall and Benton Park estates lay alongside each other to the north of the Coast Road and to the west of Red Hall Drive. The 1865 Ordnance Survey Map shows Benton Hall as being called Little Benton House. Name changes were as common then as they are today and a change of ownership could often result in a change of name.

Benton Hall survived its close neighbour, Benton Park, by about ten years but finally was also lost to residential development in about 1950.

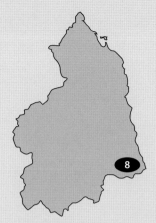

Benton Park

BENTON. *c.1780 - c.1938.*

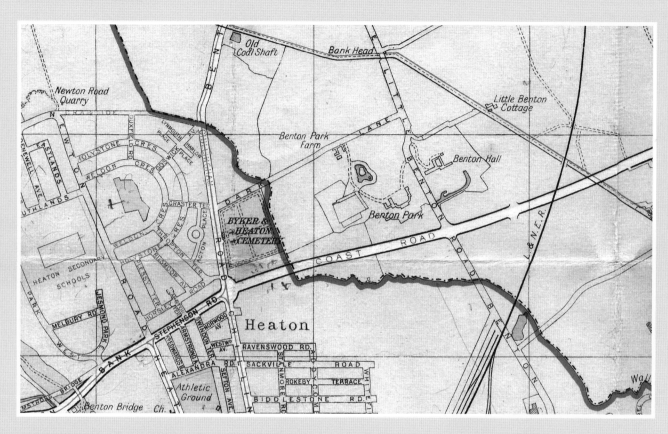

A stylish house, Benton Park's main block was joined to its wings by curved walls which together formed a grand entrance front.

The eastward expansion of Newcastle's suburbs ensured the rapid covering of its grounds in residential development immediately after the house's demolition in 1938.

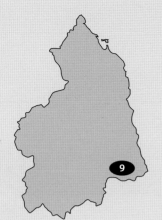

Benwell Cottage

BENWELL. *1844 - 1972.*

Benwell was only integrated into the city of Newcastle in 1904. Its favoured position in countryside just to the west of the city made it a magnet for the newly wealthy middle classes to build their grand houses and miniature estates. One of these people was civil engineer, William Hawthorn, who built Benwell Cottage in 1844. Much of the estate was sold off to house builders in the 1930s. The cottage itself became a young men's hostel for the Royal Victoria School for the Blind before being demolished in 1972.

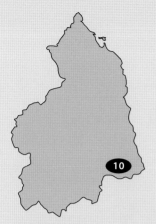

Benwell Grove

BENWELL. *1816 - c.1915.*

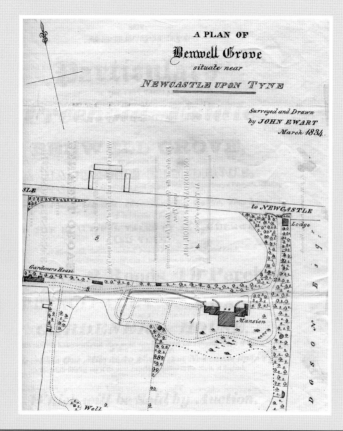

A PLAN OF
Benwell Grove
situate near
NEWCASTLE UPON TYNE

*Surveyed and Drawn
by JOHN EWART
March 1834.*

Particulars
OF THE VERY VALUABLE
Freehold Estate
OF
BENWELL GROVE,
CONSISTING OF
A HANDSOME RESIDENCE,
Placed on a Commanding Eminence, and affording the most extensive and highly picturesque Prospects, including a View of
Axwell Park, Gibside, Ravensworth Castle, Durham Cathedral,
AND THE BEAUTIFUL VALES OF TYNE, DERWENT, AND TEAM,
With Shrubberies, Gardens, Orchard, Planted Pleasure Grounds, and Lands,
COMPRISING ALTOGETHER A BEAUTIFUL DOMAIN OF
17 Acres, 2 Roods, 19 Perches,
(OR THEREABOUTS,)
PRINCIPALLY IN GRASS;
ALSO A
GARDENER'S HOUSE,
With BREWHOUSE, LAUNDRY, and other useful detached Offices and a plentiful Supply of Spring Water, of most excellent quality,
Situate within One Mile and a Half from Newcastle upon Tyne.
The whole forming one of the most desirable Situations in the North of England,

Which will be Sold by Auction,
BY
MR JOHN EWART,
AT THE QUEEN'S HEAD INN,
Newcastle upon Tyne,
On Monday the 31st Day of March, 1834, at 12 o'Clock at Noon,
(By Order of the Assignees of Mr Anthony Clapham, a Bankrupt.)

The Property may be viewed on applying at the House, and printed Particulars, with Plan of the Estate, had at

Designed by Dobson in 1816, the sale plan explains why Benwell was such a popular site for the villas of Newcastle's wealthy businessmen.

"Placed on a commanding eminence, and affording the most extensive and highly picturesque prospects, including a view of Axwell Park, Gibside, Ravensworth Castle, Durham Cathedral."

Perhaps the later additions of the Redheugh Gas Works and Dunston Power Station made the view a little less attractive.

Benwell Hall

BENWELL. *c.1750 - 1982.*

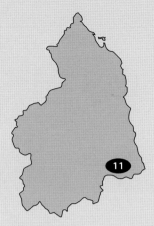

Unusually for a county which traditionally prefers stone
for its large houses, Benwell Hall was built with brick.
The original five bay centre was built in 1750 but its non-
symmetrical wings were clearly added at different times.
Other brick country houses still survive in Northumberland,
the late seventeenth century Higham Dykes, north of
Ponteland is a good example.

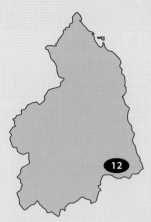

Benwell House

BENWELL. *c.1820 - 1972.*

Poor old Benwell House ended its days as a public house surrounded by residential development. It was demolished in 1972 and a chapel of rest built on its site. Its close surviving neighbour, Benwell Tower, is now also a public house called 'The Mitre' following a period of use as the residence of the Bishops of Newcastle. Such is often the fate of country houses consumed by ever growing suburbs.

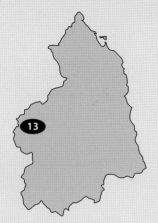

Bewshaugh

KEILDER *c.1850 - 1982 (under Keilder Reservoir)*

For generations the home of the Hedley family who played
an important role in the social life of the North Tyne Valley.
The Hedley's shared a pack of hounds with the Robson
family of Willowbog and organised social events at Keilder
culminating in the Hunt Ball. Together with Mounces,
Whickhope Lodge, Otterstone Lee and several other houses,
the remains of Bewshaugh now lie under Keilder Water.

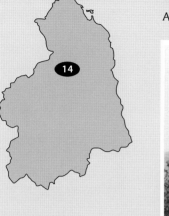

Biddlestone Hall

ALWINTON. *c.1350 – rebuilt and enlarged 1796-1957*

14

Home to the Selby family for almost seven hundred years, the family chapel built from the original pele tower is the only survivor of Biddlestone Hall. The house was used as a convalescent home during the Second World War as were so many other country houses throughout the country. An old tradition claims that Biddlestone inspired the creation of Walter Scott's Osbaldestone Hall in his 'Rob Roy'.

Birdhope Craig

ROCHESTER. *1682. Rebuilt c.1850 - 1963.*

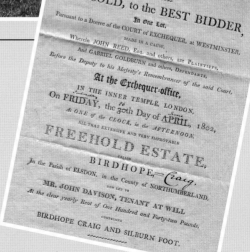

The date stone of 1682 on the kennel block at Birdhope Craig reminds us that an earlier house than that shown above once existed. The later house built as a shooting box for the Earl of Redesdale, served a huge twenty six thousand acre estate which reached northward to the Scottish border. In 1911, the Hall and almost three thousand acres were sold to the War Office to form an army training area. The house burnt down in 1963 and is survived by outbuildings and a lodge.

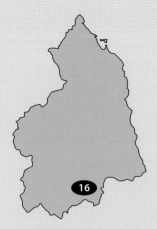

16

Black Hedley (Gatehouse)

KILN PIT HILL. *1750 - 1964.*

16

The Georgian house at Black Hedley still stands but its
castellated gatehouse pictured was demolished in 1964.
The cottages to either side of the gatehouse survive as do the
figures surmounting it which can now be seen on the gate
piers of Shotley Hall, also in Northumberland.

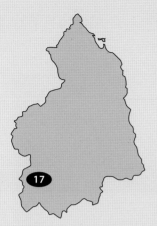

Blenkinsopp Castle

BLENKINSOPP. *1339. Added to 1830s. Rebuilt and enlarged 1880 -1954.*

The seat of the old Northumberland family of Blenkinsopp from the 1200s until 1727, when the estate passed by marriage to John Coulson of Jesmond Manor House, also now demolished. In the early 1830s, John Dobson designed a small castellated house to join the original pele tower. This was replaced in 1880 by a Tudor gothic country house designed by William Glover. In 1954, this house was gutted by fire and remains a ruin. Part of the original pele tower survives as the centre of a chalet park.

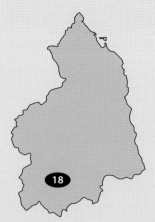

Bonny Rigg Hall

BARDON MILL. *1829 - 1985.*

Sir Edward Blackett's diary entry for New Year's Day, 1829, reads:

"Went to Gallowshield Rigg with Mr Dobson and fixed upon a situation for a shooting box."

The resulting Bonny Rigg Hall proved to be one of the grandest shooting boxes in Northumberland. It was used by the Blackett's for shooting and holidays until the 1930s. It was owned by them until 1968 and burnt down in 1985. It is survived by a stable block wing shown to the far left in the above view which has been converted into two cottages.

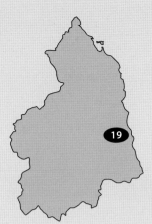

Bothal Haugh

BOTHAL. *1880 - ?*

19

Bothal Haugh was built as a privately owned rectory by the Hon. and Rev. William Charles Ellis. He had the distinction of being Rector of Bothal for sixty two years from 1861 until 1923. As the son of Lord Howard De Walden, his house, Bothal Haugh, clearly expressed the status and prestige of a well connected and well placed Victorian clergyman.

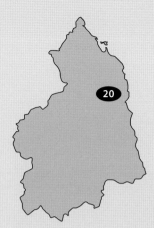

20

Broom Park

BOLTON. *c.1660. Extended c.1750 - 1953.*

20

From 1658 until the early twentieth century, Broom Park was the seat of the Burrell family. Probably designed by William Newton, the house was altered in 1829 by John Dobson for William Burrell. Dobson had a reputation for being able to make old houses more comfortable by eliminating draughts and worked to this end on many of Northumberland's large houses.

Bygate Hall

ALWINTON. *c.1800 - 1952.*

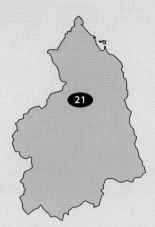

Bygate Hall was the centre of a two thousand acre farm occupied in the first half of the twentieth century by the Cowen family. The many fire places in the house in this remote part of Northumberland all burned peat dug by farm labourers from nearby Philhope Edge. Bygate Hall was last occupied in 1940, demolished in 1952, and replaced by Bygate Cottages.

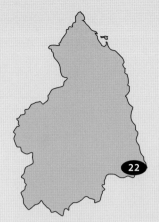

Carville Hall

WALLSEND. *1635. Rebuilt c.1750 - 1898.*

Built in 1635 for John Cosyn, a Newcastle merchant
and alderman, as a country retreat. Cosyn also had a
magnificent Elizabethan town house on Newcastle Quayside,
unfortunately destroyed in the Great Fire of 1854. Carville
had extensive grounds and as industry began to encroach on
the once rural scene, a sun dial with the Cosyn Arms dated
1667 was given to the Society of Antiquaries and placed in
Newcastle Keep. Robert Carr had the Hall rebuilt in 1750
and with its seventy acres of grounds intact it survived until
1898. Terrace housing covered the site.

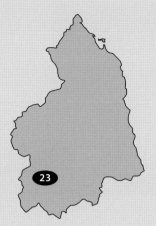

Castle Hill Pele

HALTWHISTLE. *1611. Extended 1680 - 1963.*

Built by Albany Featherstonehaugh in 1611 near to the site of the original Motte and Bailey Castle of Haltwhistle.

The central tower was built first with walls between three and five feet thick. Although the English and Scottish Crowns were joined in 1603, Haltwhistle was still a lawless place. The east wing was added soon after building and in 1680, further extensions were carried out. In 1870, the whole building was re-roofed and the original stone roof flags were found to have been laid on oak beams and fastened in place with sheep shank bones.

The Chase

COWPEN. *c.1750 - 1960s.*

Along with demolished Cowpen Hall, Cowpen House and
Cowpen Grove - Chase House gave Cowpen Road an air of
Georgian grandeur and respectability. Unfortunately, all
these houses disappeared in the 1960s and their gardens
and grounds were used for housing development.

Chirton House

CHIRTON. c.1650. Extended 1693 - 1899.

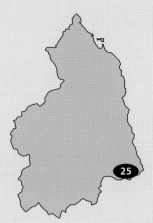

The grand five bay block to the right of the picture was added in 1693 to the original smaller house shown to the left. Built by the Milbourne family, it became the seat of the Collingwood's in the late eighteenth century. Its most famous owner was Admiral Lord Collingwood. He never lived here spending most of his life at sea but it was home to Lady Collingwood and their daughter.

Condercum House

BENWELL. *c.1870 – c.1938.*

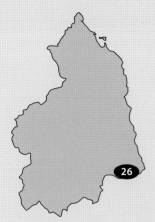

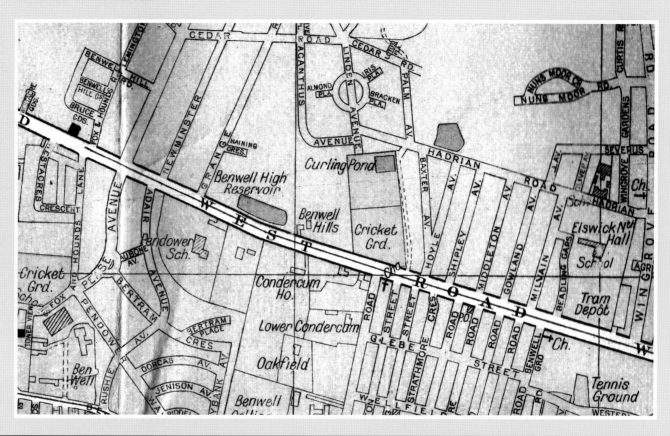

The Condercum estate sale plans of 1934 show a nineteen acre site with three large detached houses; Condercum House, Condercum Villa and Oakfield. All three houses have now gone and the site is now covered with houses built in the 1940s and 1950s. The sale plans were accurate to a degree by describing the site as –

"being ripe for development as a modern building estate"

Condercum House itself was –

"a brick-built residence of superior construction, containing three reception rooms, eight bedrooms, two bathrooms, cloakroom with lavatory, kitchen and domestic offices, stabling, garages, outbuildings and two cottages."

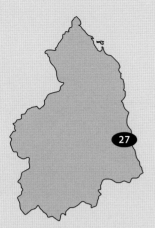

Cowpen Grove

COWPEN. *c.1750 - 1960s.*

 27

A stylish three storey Georgian house with a splendid door case, originally set in fine gardens and grounds which gradually were used for building terraces of houses.

Cowpen Hall

COWPEN. *1686. Rebuilt 1720 - 1958.*

Home of the Sidney family from 1729 until the middle of
the twentieth century. James Lees-Milne tells us in his diaries
of 1944-1945:

*"Mama made me drive her to Broadway to see the Sidney's
Flemish primitives and Tudor family portraits which, I
gathered, they had just discovered in their Northumberland
house, Cowpen Hall"*

Cowpen Hall was leased from the Sidney family during
the 1930s.

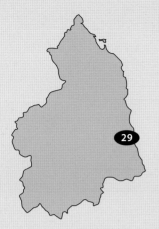

Cowpen House

COWPEN. *c.1750 - c.1970.*

The 1886 directory lists the occupants of Cowpen House as being Miss Susan and Miss Mary Ann Sidney. Their brother, Henry Sidney esquire J.P., is shown as occupying Cowpen Hall at the same date, so perhaps Cowpen House filled the role of Dower House for the Sidney family. After its demolition in 1970, the house was replaced by the Cowpen and Bebside British Legion Club building.

Coxlodge Hall

GOSFORTH. *1796. Rebuilt 1877 -1939.*

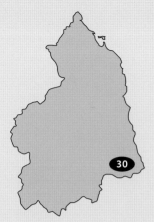

Built for a Mr Job Bulman who made his fortune in India and gave his name to that part of Gosforth still known as Bulman Village. Much of the estate had been sold by the early 1930s for expensive suburban development.

By the time the second picture was taken, the house was being used as a private school called Smart's College. It was demolished in 1939 and is survived by its lodge and stable block now being used as commercial premises.

Cresswell Hall

CRESSWELL. *1821/25 - 1937.*

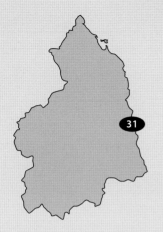

Like the Craster's, Roddam's and Widdrington's, the Cresswell family had held their Northumberland estates from the twelfth century onwards. Their original tower house at Cresswell still survives but the grand classical wing added to it in the 1750s was demolished in 1845.

The house, built for the family between 1821 and 1825, by the nationally important architect, John Shaw, was demolished in 1937. Shaw had visited Belsay Hall whilst it was under construction and this obviously greatly influenced his design of Cresswell.

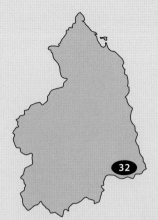

Cross House

NEWCASTLE – CLAREMONT ROAD. c.1840 - 1960.

Cross House shown above shares its name with two other lost Newcastle houses.

High Cross House, designed by John Dobson and built in 1851 in Benwell, was demolished in 1906, and replaced by housing and shops.

The older Cross House, built opposite the central station in around 1700, was demolished in 1912. A commercial building took its place and still keeps its name alive.

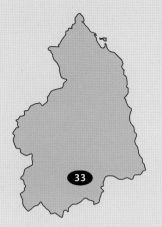

Dilston Hall

DILSTON. *1400s. Enlarged 1616, rebuilt 1714 - 1767.*

Dilston Hall was famous as the home of James Radcliffe, third Earl of Derwent Water. A leader in the Jacobite Rebellion, he was attainted of High Treason and beheaded on Tower Hill in 1716. He was buried at Dilston but his remains were moved to Thorndon Hall, Essex, in 1874. His forfeited estates passed to the Trustees of Greenwich Hospital and in 1765 the Board of Commissioners ordered that:

"The house be entirely taken down."

The high stone wall in the left foreground and the bridge to the right still survive.

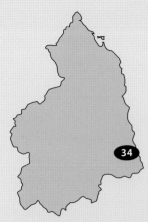

Earsdon White House

EARSDON. *c.1680. Refaced c.1780 - 1959.*

For generations the home of the Barker family who re-faced
the house in the late seventeen hundreds on inheriting some
family money. The house was commandeered during the
First World War and used as an officers' mess. In later years
it became the home of Earsdon Working Men's Club before
its demolition in 1959.

Elswick Hall

ELSWICK. *c.1400. Rebuilt 1803 - 1977.*

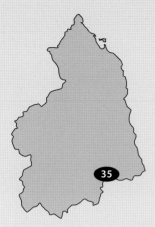

Elswick Hall was built in 1803 on the site of the earlier tower house by the Newcastle architect, William Stokoe and his partner and son, John. Bruce's Handbook to Newcastle tells us that:

"After Anderson Place Mr Grainger purchased a large estate in the west of the town, the Elswick Estate. He said, 'I will not stop until I have made Elswick Hall the centre of Newcastle'."

Grainger ran into financial difficulties which stopped his development plans but the hall survived until 1977 after being used for a time as a museum. Elswick swimming pool now occupies its site.

Elswick House

ELSWICK. *c.1820 - 1984.*

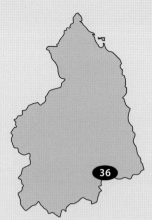

36

36

Looking much like a miniature version of Cresswell Hall
and built at almost the same time, Elswick House was
typical of the many early villas which sprang up in the leafy
suburbs of Newcastle. Built by the newly rich merchants and
industrialists of the booming city, Elswick House survived
as a private home until the 1930s. After a decade's use as a
children's home, it became St. Anne's Convent High School in
the late 1940s. It was demolished in 1984 and its site is now
occupied by the Marie Curie Centre.

Felton Park

FELTON. *1732. Rebuilt 1747 - 1952.*

FELTON PARK from the S? WEST
North.ᵈ
The Seat of Ralph Riddell Esq.ʳ
Published Nov.ʳ 1827. by W. Davison Alnwick

For long the home of the Widdrington family and passed through marriage to the Riddels, Felton Park has played a major role in the history of Roman Catholicism in Northumberland. Sykes 'Historical Records' tell us:

"1747, January 24th, at ten o'clock in the morning a fire broke out, which burnt with great violence, and in four hours consumed the body of the house."

The house was rebuilt and in 1799 a new east wing was added. After demolition of the main block this wing now forms the present Felton Park. It can be seen above in the right hand background of the lost house of 1747, which was demolished in 1952.

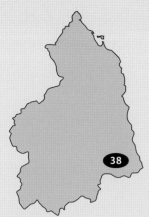

Forest Hall

FOREST HALL. c.1500. Centre block c.1730. Balancing right-hand wing 1800s - 1962.

Forest Hall started life as a medieval tower house shown
to the left of the picture. The five bay centre block was
added circa 1730 and the right hand wing was added in the
late eighteen hundreds to give symmetry to the hall front.
Frequently tenanted during the nineteenth century, the
house was once again occupied by the Wilson family from
1910 until 1956. Their ancestors had built the central 1730s
block. The site is now covered with housing.

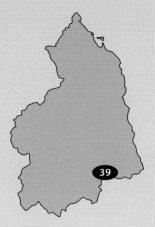

The Gables (later Hopedean House)

ELSWICK. *c.1850 - 1996.*

Built by the Quaker Richardson family, owners of nearby
Elswick Leather Works, the Gables later had its name
changed to Hopedean House. In the 1920s, the house
became a private nursing home and many Tynesiders were
born here. The Gables ended its days as a Salvation Army
hostel and its Richardson owners still live in Northumberland
at Wheelbirks near Stocksfield.

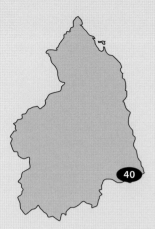

The Grange

WALLSEND. *c.1750 - 1910.*

40

One of several imposing houses fronting the village green at Wallsend including Wallsend Hall and the lost Red House and White House. The 'History of the Parish of Wallsend' tells us:

"It was a large house of fourteen rooms with dairy, laundry, byres etc. This was the mansion house of the middle farm estate consisting of one hundred and twenty-four acres."

The house survived until 1910 and in 1913 Grange Villas were build on the site.

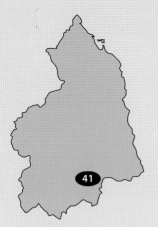

Grey Court

RIDING MILL. *c.1875 - 1940.*

Originally known as Willow Wood House and re-named Grey Court by Sir Alexander Leith, whose home it was from 1914 until the early 1920s. In 1936 the house was given to the Royal Victoria Infirmary for use as a convalescent home by Mr Newall of nearby Shepherd's Dene. The house burnt to the ground in 1940 and a smaller house now occupies the magnificent Victorian terrace on which Grey Court used to sit. The glorious specimen trees planted by earlier owners provide a magnificent setting.

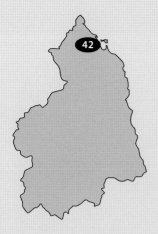

Haggerston Castle

HAGGERSTON. *c.1200. Rebuilt 1618. Rebuilt 1777. Added to 1808. Rebuilt 1892 - 97. Rebuilt 1911/12 - 1933.*

Without doubt the most rebuilt house in Northumberland, Haggerston Castle must also have been one of the largest. It also has a complicated architectural history.

The central seven bay block (top-left picture). shows the house built by Sir Thomas Haggerston in 1777, replacing the earlier house of 1618. In 1808 this house was extended by two three storey bays to the left and right of the main block. The house was bought by the Naylor-Leyland family in 1858 and between 1892 and 1897, Norman Shaw was commissioned to almost double the size of the house but keeping the existing front unchanged.

Disastrously, this vast Georgian-Victorian pile burnt down in 1911. Undeterred the Naylor-Leyland's commissioned James Dunn of Edinburgh to build a new house (which is shown top-right) at an enormous cost.

The house only survived for another twenty years. The famous five day demolition sale of 1931 resulted in most of the garden balustrading and stonework being rebuilt forty miles away at Holystone Grange. Mrs Lee acquired stonework and interior fittings which helped her build West Martin near Wooler. Many other Northumberland houses contain bits of poor old Haggerston Castle.

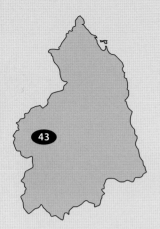

Hawkhope Hill

FALSTONE.

Bulmer's 'History of Northumberland' of 1886 tells us:

"Hawkhope Hill, the residence of Mr Matthew Atkinson Ridley, occupies a commanding situation on the north side of Falstone. About the middle of the sixteenth century it was the property of Jasper Charlton of whom it was recorded."

"The Laird of Hakupe, whose name was Charlton, was slaine on Friday last in Jedwart Forest in Stealinge. Ane tuik him by the heid and dang out all his harnes."

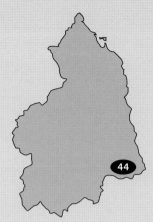

Heaton Hall

HEATON. *c.1600. Rebuilt 1713. Rebuilt 1770 - 1933.*

Rebuilt in 1770 by William Newton for the White-Ridley family now represented by the Ridley's of Blagdon Hall. Indeed the circular temple which the Ridley's moved from Heaton to Blagdon is the only reminder of this lost house. Not everyone admired its light pastry-cook Gothic style which spread throughout the county following the Duke of Northumberland's Gothicising of Alnwick Castle. Cecelia Ridley tells us:

"With his newly acquired wealth Richard Ridley bought a large estate at Heaton. Here he built a large, and for the period, curiously ugly mansion".

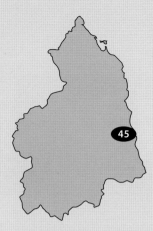

Hirst Castle

ASHINGTON. *1536. Rebuilt 1700s - 1908.*

Hirst Castle survived until 1908 when the ever expanding coal mining town of Ashington saw its demolition for road widening and housing development. The Trollope style front of the early 1700s had been added to the tower of 1536. The resulting Northumbrian vernacular building was typical of the many minor houses which have disappeared in the county.

Jesmond Dean

JESMOND. *1835 - c.1935.*

46

Jesmond Dean was one of several grand houses built in
the Ouseburn Valley. Not to be confused with Jesmond
Dene House which still survives as a hotel and restaurant,
the house was built in 1835 for the twenty five year old
solicitor, William George Armstrong, in preparation for his
forthcoming marriage. William was later to become famous
as Lord Armstrong of Cragside. The site is now covered by the
houses of Glastonbury and Castleton Grove.

Jesmond Grove

JESMOND. *c.1795 - 1927.*

From 1916 until its demolition in 1927, Jesmond Grove housed boarders from Newcastle Church High School. This earlier view shows the indoor staff of owner and brewer W.B. Reid, in 1906.

The message on the reverse of this early postcard view is typical of many in my collection. Sent home to mother it says:

"This is a view of the house I am working at at present."

So many people worked in service at this time and postcards were the cheapest way of keeping in touch with family and friends.

Jesmond Manor House

JESMOND.   *1720. Rebuilt c.1830 - 1929.*

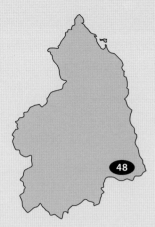

Many Haldane tells us in 'A Record of a Hundred Years 1825-1925':

"The manor house of Jesmond was pronounced to be in a dangerous condition owing to the undermining of the colliery, and it was entirely rebuilt and a new foundation stone laid."

Many Haldane was unique in living in three of the lost houses pictured in this book. Her father hired both Otterburn Dene and Biddlestone Hall during the time it took for his new house, Jesmond Dene House, to be completed.

Like many other houses illustrated in this book, its site was developed for housing.

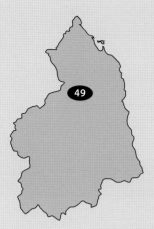

Kidland

KIDLAND. *1896 - 1957.*

Built by Christopher John Naylor Leyland of Haggerston Castle at about the same time that he was doubling the size of the Castle and spending enormous sums of money on both.

At one thousand two hundred and fifty feet above sea level, Kidland was the highest placed shooting lodge in England.

After standing empty for over twenty years, the house was demolished in 1957. Only the stable block survives to remind us of this most isolated and dramatically sited house.

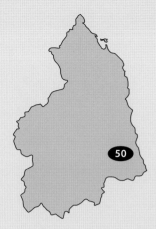

Killingworth House

KILLINGWORTH. *c.1760. Bow window bays added 1770s - 1956.*

Killingworth was designed by Lancelot Coxon for the Roddam family. They also employed him to make alterations to Roddam Hall, their seat south of Wooler. Roddam still survives although it did loose its second floor in a reduction exercise in 1979.

The better known architect, William Newton made alterations to Killingworth House in the 1770s, probably the bow window bays to either side of the main block.

Low Gosforth House

GOSFORTH. *1852. Rebuilt 1878 - 1970s.*

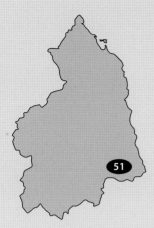

Originally a secondary house on the Gosforth Park estate, Low Gosforth was the home of Robert William Brandling. His elder brother, Ralph Henry Brandling resided in the much grander Gosforth House.

The Brandling's sold the whole estate in 1852 and Low Gosforth with three hundred acres was bought by Joseph Laycock for £28,600. He proceeded to rebuild the house which was rebuilt a second time in 1878 after a disastrous fire. This house survived until the 1970s when it was replaced by the houses of the Melton Park estate.

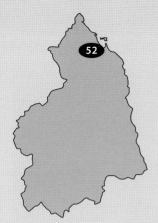

Low Lynn

KYLOE. *c.1750 - ruinous.*

52

Low Lynn was a mid-eighteenth century five bay house shown to the right of the picture. The buildings to the left are nineteenth century extensions. The house assumed its present ruinous condition after standing empty for many years.

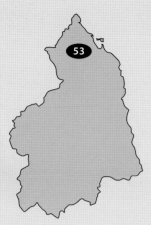

Milfield Hill

MILFIELD. *c.1760. Rebuilt c.1830 - 1967.*

The early Victorian house illustrated replaced the mid-eighteenth century house of the Grey family. John Grey recorded that his father, George, who died in 1789:

"Took an axe and, like a backwood settler, cut away the broom and cleared for himself a space in which to begin his farming function."

John Grey was the father of the famous Reformer, Josephine Butler.

The house was used by Royal Air Force personnel during the Second World War and was demolished in 1967.

Mitford Manor House

MITFORD. c.1550. East front remodelled and tower added 1637. Mostly demolished 1812.

54

The second of three houses built on the Mitford estate but all built in different locations. The original Motte and Bailey Castle of the twelfth century survives as a ruin. So does the remodelled sixteenth century manor house shown right. Thankfully, John Dobson's Mitford Hall of 1828 survives.

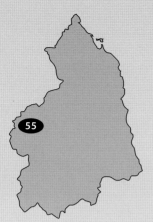

Mounces

PLASHETTS. *c.1800 - 1982 (under Kielder Water).*

55

Mounces was built as a shooting box for Sir John Swinburne at the centre of a seventeen thousand acre estate, which was considered one of the best grouse moors in Northern England.

The nine bedroomed lodge was serviced by staff that lived in the building visible to the left of the picture.

Mounces was later used to house Keilder forestry workers and now lies below the Kielder Reservoir.

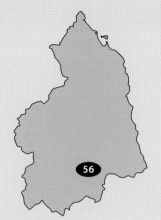

Nesbitt

OUSTON. *c.1860 - c.1940.*

Nesbitt was demolished at the start of the Second World
War to make way for the airfield at Ouston. The Elizabethan
architectural details of this Victorian farmhouse are untypical
of the normally much plainer Northumberland style.

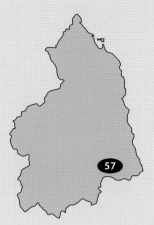

Newbiggin Hall

WESTERHOPE. *Rebuilt c.1800 -1950s.*

From 1909, Newbiggin Hall was the home of Gerald France and his wife, Hilda May. Hilda was the eldest of the eight children of Thomas Hudson Bainbridge of the famous Newcastle department store. They had moved to Newbiggin from Horsley House near Wylam and Hilda remained there until her death in 1954. The house was demolished shortly after this and replaced by a public house which contained a few fittings from the Hall. The pub has since been demolished and the only reminder is the name of the area as Newbiggin Hall estate.

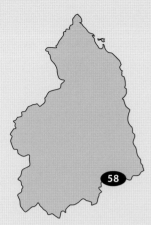

Newburn Manor House

NEWBURN. *c.1600 - 1909.*

58

Nothing remains in Newburn of the seventeenth century
manor house with its typical mullioned windows and
pantiled roof with its lower courses of stone tiles. However, in
neighbouring County Durham, two fireplaces removed from
Newburn can be seen reinstated at Washington Old Hall.

The house was demolished in 1909 to enable road widening
and industrial development.

North Seaton Hall

SEATON SLUICE. *1710 - c.1960.*

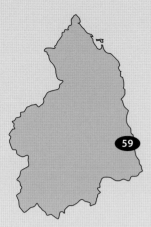

In a *'Memoir of John Dobson'*, his daughter, Margaret Jane, claims North Seaton Hall as his first design of 1813. Although Dobson may have worked here in 1813, the house was built in 1710, for the Watson family whose home it remained for several generations. Dobson definitely worked on the house in 1831. Nikolaus Pevsner found North Seaton *"very neglected"* in the 1950s and it was demolished c1960.

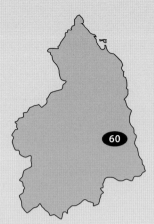

Orde House

MORPETH. *1715 - 1967.*

Orde House was built in 1715 for Mr Orde, Governor of Morpeth's House of Correction, which itself was replaced by John Dobson's County Gaol complex which still dominates this part of Morpeth. The Governor's house survived but was divided up into several dwellings. It was finally demolished in 1967.

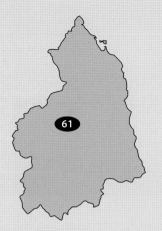

Otterburn Dene

OTERBURN. *c.1970.*

61

Otterburn Dene was demolished c.1970 and its estate incorporated into an army camp and firing range. The house's isolation is described by Mary Haldane as:

"The shooting lodge in which we lived so much - Otterburn Dene - is situated in the midst of moorland, and as there is only one road to it we had to go round a long way or ride over the moor."

NORTHUMBERLAND

(IN THE BORDER HUNT)

2 miles from Otterburn, 7½ from Woodburn Station, 9 miles from Bellingham Station, 35 miles from Newcastle-upon-Tyne, 80 miles from Edinburgh

A VERY ATTRACTIVE

FREEHOLD PASTORAL AND SPORTING PROPERTY

KNOWN AS

Otterburn Dene Estate

EXTENDING TO AN AREA OF ABOUT

2674 ACRES

AND HAVING AN ANNUAL RENTAL VALUE OF

£856, 2s.

INCLUDING THE DESIRABLE RESIDENCE

OTTERBURN DENE HOUSE AND GROUNDS

ALSO THE FARMS OF

DAVYSHIELDS, HOPEFOOT, HOPEHEAD, & THE RAW

Four noted Sheep Farms with well-built Homesteads

AN IDEAL SPORTING ESTATE affording excellent Grouse and Blackgame Shooting over the well-known Davyshield Moor; also Pheasant, Partridge, and Wild-fowl. Trout Fishing in the River Otter, and Hunting with the celebrated Border Pack.

To be Exposed for Sale by Public Roup

By Mr WM. PARLOUR

WITHIN THE COUNTY HOTEL, NEWCASTLE-UPON-TYNE
(unless previously Sold by Private Bargain)

ON TUESDAY, THE 27TH DAY OF MAY 1919, AT 2.30 P.M. PROMPT

Plans and Particulars may be obtained by application to the Auctioneer at his Office, Croft, Darlington; or to Messrs LINDSAY, JAMIESON & HALDANE, C.A., 24 St. Andrew Square, Edinburgh; Messrs NEISH, HOWELL & HALDANE, Solicitors, 47 Watling Street, London, E.C. 4; B. CLAYHILLS, Esq., Land Agent, 6 Eldon Square, Newcastle-upon-Tyne.

1

Pandon House

NEWCASTLE – PANDON BANK. *c.1750 - c.1930.*

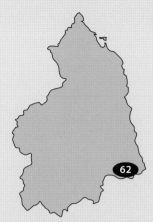

62

Situated close to the site of the long demolished medieval
Pandon Hall, poor Pandon House ended its days as a
printers' establishment. This enterprise was begun in 1925
following a long period of use of the house as a home for
destitute boys. At the bottom of its large garden stood
the Sallyport gate, the only surviving gate in Newcastle's
medieval town walls. The old village of Pandon had become
part of the town in 1298 explaining the great curve in the
town wall built to enclose it.

Paradise House

SCOTSWOOD. *c.1720 - 1958.*

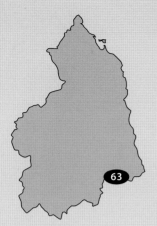

Paradise House was built to the south of the old Scotswood Road with its gardens and grounds running down to to River Tyne. In the 1830s its Arcadian site was ruined with the building of the Paradise Railway Bridge, known as the Skew Bridge, which crossed over Scotswood Road immediately behind the house. Paradise no longer.

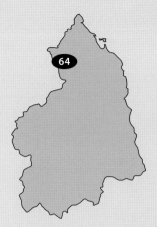

Pawston House

MINDRUM. *c.1550. Rebuilt c.1870 – ruinous.*

The Selby family who owned the Biddlestone estate for over seven hundred years were also the owners of Pawston. The house started life as a mid-sixteenth century pele tower which was extended in 1870. It remained in Selby hands until 1921 and survives as a roofless ruin.

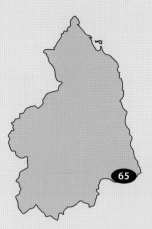

Point Pleasant House

WALLSEND. *c.1750 - ?*

WALLSEND SLIPWAY. R.C.
1911

With gardens and grounds stretching westwards to Wallsend and south to the Tyne, Point Pleasant's magnificent vistas were all lost to Victorian industry. The 1897 Ordnance Survey Map shows its once arcadian views to have been replaced by cement works, gas works, aluminium works, shipyards and docks. No wonder its owners decided to live elsewhere.

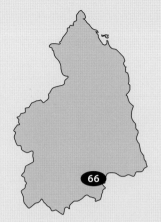

66

Prudhoe Hall – East Lodge

PRUDHOE. *1878 - ?*

66

Prudhoe Hall was built in 1878 for Matthew Liddell, the son of Cuthbert Liddell of demolished Benwell Hall. Prudhoe Hall described in Pevsner as:

"Rather formless but redeemed by much naturalistic stone carved detail."

still stands. Unusually its two lodges, the East Lodge on Moor Road and West Lodge on the A695, have both been demolished. Lodges tend to survive as their small size and generally attractive appearance appeal to many house hunters.

Ray

KIRKWHELPINGTON. *c.1880 - 1945.*

This remote Victorian house spent most of its life hosting shooting parties. Richard Burn, who eventually bought Carrycoats Hall, tells us that in his house hunting forays:

"Our first plan for setting up the marital home was to lease Ray Demesne, Kirkwhelpington. It was a somewhat large, rambling, one story house forming three sides of a courtyard. Word reached me that the War Office had requisitioned the house so the deal was off. At the end of the War the house was demolished being overwhelmed by dry rot fungus."

A lucky escape!

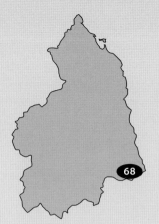

Red House

WALLSEND. *c.1770 - c.1900.*

68

The *'History of the Parish of Wallsend'* tells us the Red House was:

"A large red-brick mansion house of three stories containing over twenty rooms, with stabling, gardens etc."

Also:

"The house was next used as a cripples' home for children, who were moved from Whickham."

A new home for these children opened in Gosforth in 1897 and shortly after this the Red House was demolished.

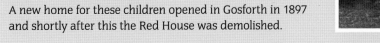

Riddlehamhope

HEXHAMSHIRE. *Mentioned as Redeleme in 1214. Extended over time, mostly demolished c.1950.*

The picture above, circa 1920, shows gamekeeper Joe Mole with the Duchess of Connaught at the back of the main house. Mainly used as a shooting lodge, Riddlehamhope was built of stone covered with harling which gave the house a Scottish air. The scant remains remind us of the impressive country house used for grand parties during the shooting season which was mostly demolished around 1950.

St. Anthony's Old Hall

NEWCASTLE – ST. ANTHONY'S. *1620 - ?*

Built in 1620 by the devout Roman Catholic, Dame Dorothy Lawson. Having a private chapel in regular use in the house, the Dame escaped the penalties suffered by other Northern recusants. Her family connections and good works placed her in such high regard that her funeral barge was met at Newcastle Quayside in 1638 with:

"The streets shining with tapers as light as if it had been noon. The Magistrates and Aldermen with the whole glory of the place attended at the landing place to wait on the coffin."

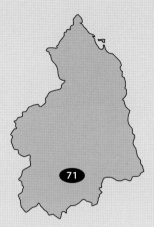

St. Wilfrid's

HEXHAM. *c.1865 - 1995.*

Built for Attorney, Richard Gibson, and lived in by his
son, Jasper until his death in 1917. Purchased in 1919, by
Hexham War Memorial Committee and opened as a cottage
hospital by Prince Henry, later Duke of Gloucester, on 29th
September 1921. When its closure was announced, plans
were made to purchase the building and make it a care
centre. Despite strong local disapproval, it was demolished
and replaced by housing in 1995.

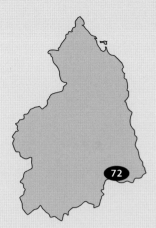

Scotswood House

SCOTSWOOD. *c.1800 - 1970's.*

Bulmer's Directory of 1887, shows Scotswood House as being the residence of John Macleod Campbell. He was a Director of Stephenson and Co. Ltd., Locomotive builders and makers of marine engines. By 1860, this company was the largest employer on Tyneside.

The house went in the late 1970s, a victim of the development of a new road system which also saw the demolition of neighbouring Scotswood Tower.

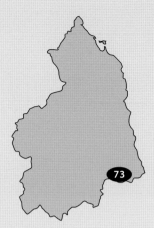

Scotswood Tower

SCOTSWOOD. *c.1350 - Victorian additions - 1981.*

Many travelers will remember Scotswood Tower with its commanding position overlooking the old Scotswood Bridge. named after Richard Scot, who owned the wooded land here in the mid-1300s and who probably had the old pele tower built. This was altered and extended in Victorian times with the tower given new windows and crenellation.

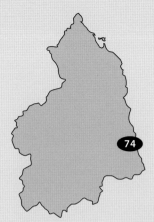

Seaton Lodge

SEATON SLUICE. *1670 - 1970s.*

Sir John Delaval of nearby Seaton Delaval Hall described
Seaton Lodge as:

"The finest thatched house in the kingdom."

Other family members must have held the same view because
in 1682, Sir Ralph Delaval entertained the famous diarist,
Samuel Pepys, at Seaton Lodge. Pepys was described as 'The
Architect of Royal Navy Administration' and this visit may
account for Sir Ralph's promotion to vice admiral in 1690.

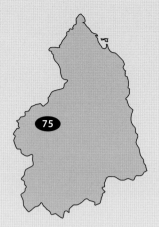

Sidwood

GREENHAUGH. *c.1720 - 1966.*

Situated in the centre of a two thousand acre estate which
for a long time was home to the Watson family. The house
was left empty for several years before being set alight. When
it was finally demolished in 1966 the land was purchased by
the Forestry Commission who planted the area with trees. The
photograph clearly shows the original Georgian farmhouse to
the left with the larger scaled Victorian additions to the right.

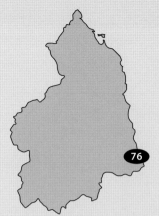

76

Sparrow Hall

CULLERCOATS. *1682 - 1979.*

76

Although built nearly a century later than Doddington,
pictured in the introduction, Sparrow Hall followed the
pattern of the traditional Northumberland strong house.
It was built by Thomas and Elizabeth Dove in 1682 and
they commemorated the event by having their intertwined
initials carved in stone on the finial topping the east gable.
The carving of a dove to illustrate the family name is
supposed to have resulted in the locals giving the house the
name of Sparrow Hall.

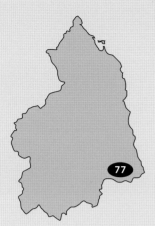

Stotes Hall

JESMOND. *1607 - 1953.*

This house was bought by Sir Richard Stote in 1658 and kept his name until its demolition in 1953. Stotes Hall was one of the earliest non-fortified manor houses in Northumberland to be built outside the town wall.

In the 1750s the house became the school of the famous Newcastle mathematician and teacher, Charles Hutton. The marble bust of himself presented to him by his pupils of over sixty years in 1822 can still be seen in the library of the Literary and Philosophical Society of Newcastle.

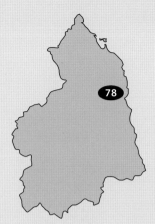

Swansfield House

ALNWICK. *1823 - c.1975.*

Designed by John Dobson in 1823 for Henry Collingwood Selby and demolished circa 1975, Swansfield has been replaced by a smaller neo-Georgian house.

The statue shown in front of the house still survives. This is the peace column erected to commemorate the peace of 1814 which now stands in the centre of Swansfield Park.

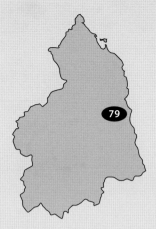

Swarland Hall

SWARLAND. *Rebuilt 1765 - 1934.*

Swarland Hall was demolished in 1934, but its near neighbour, Swarland Old Hall, designed by Robert Trollope in the 1660s still survives.

Alexander Davison, who owned the estate in the nineteenth century, shared a friendship with Admiral Lord Nelson. He erected the Nelson Monument and planted trees in the park at Swarland to represent the position of the fleets in the Battle of the Nile.

The site is now covered by expensive housing.

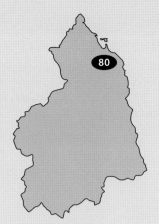

Tillmouth Park

TWIZELL. *1810 - 1880.*

Tillmouth Park was rebuilt in 1810 by Sir Francis Blake II after selling his old house, Fowberry Tower. As well as his building work at Tillmouth he was still working on the nearby, and never to be completed, Twizell Castle. Tillmouth Park, as illustrated, survived until 1880 when it was replaced by the present Victorian house of the same name. The lodges and garden features of the earlier lost house still survive as do many of the grand fire places which were re-used in the new house of 1882.

Troughend Hall

OTTERBURN. *c.1300. Rebuilt c.1740 - 1952.*

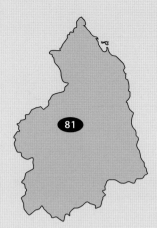

Seat of the Reed family, the most prominent in Redesdale, for almost 800 years. The eighteenth century house replaced the original pele tower, a centre of much border reiving.

Edward Keith's *'The Keeper of the Rede'*, gives an atmospheric account of life here in the 1460s.

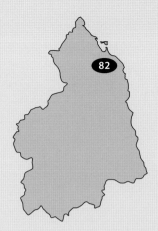

Twizell Castle

TWIZELL. *Rebuilt 1768 - c.1880.*

An ivy covered ruin is the only reminder of the vast house that took four generations of the Blake family to build. As late as 1852, James Raine claimed that the house resembled:

"An unseemly mass of unfinished masonry."

and:

"A memorial of the most extreme want of taste."

In describing the loss of Tillmouth Park another lost Northumberland house of the Blake family, Sir Roy Strong says:

"Sir Francis Blake's nightmare of a house looked across to his equally loony Twizell Castle."

The present Blake House on the estate is the delightful Gothic Dower House converted in 1976 by Felix Kelly for Sir Francis Blake.

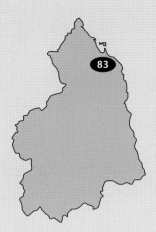

Twizell House

WARENFORD. *c.1750. Portico added 1890 - 1969/70.*

Bought in 1790 by George Selby with its seven hundred acre estate for his son, the famous gentleman Naturalist, Prideaux John Selby.

At this time there were five servants living in: the butler, footman, cook, housemaid and dairymaid. The gardener, wood keeper, lodge keeper and several agricultural labourers all lived in cottages on the estate. The Selby's remained at Twizell until 1892.

Tynemouth House

TYNEMOUTH. *c.1850 - ?*

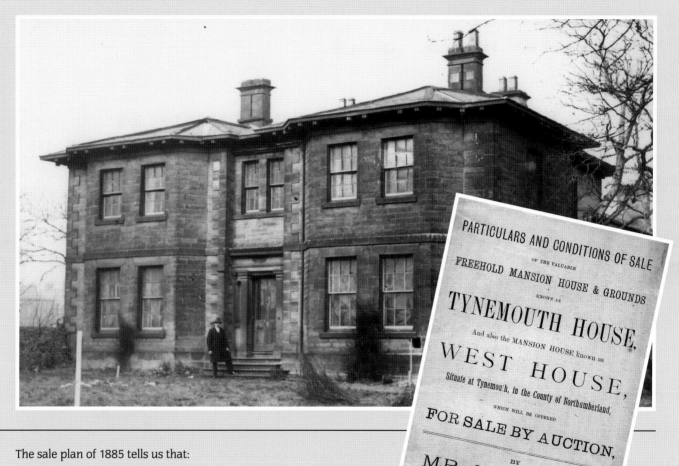

The sale plan of 1885 tells us that:

"Tynemouth House comprises a capacious entrance hall, reception rooms, library, business rooms, music room, marble Turkish bath, bedrooms, kitchens, sculleries, etc. containing in all about twenty four apartments and useful store rooms and attics. There are extensive gardens and pleasure grounds, a gardener's cottage and stables and coach houses."

PARTICULARS AND CONDITIONS OF SALE

OF THE VALUABLE

FREEHOLD MANSION HOUSE & GROUNDS

KNOWN AS

TYNEMOUTH HOUSE,

And also the MANSION HOUSE known as

WEST HOUSE,

Situate at Tynemouth, in the County of Northumberland,

WHICH WILL BE OFFERED

FOR SALE BY AUCTION,

BY

MR. JOS. WRAY,

AT THE

ROYAL TURK'S HEAD HOTEL,

GREY STREET, NEWCASTLE-UPON-TYNE,

On Wednesday, May 27th, 1885,

AT THREE O'CLOCK IN THE AFTERNOON,

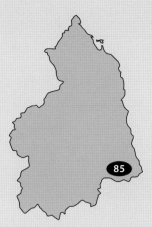

West Jesmond House

JESMOND. *c.1850 - 1970.*

Home to the brewer T. W. Lovibond, who in 1891 added a vinery
to his house to join his existing fernery and two conservatories.
In 1934 a Miss Taylor turned the house into the private Northern
Womens Hospital , changing its name to Lynton House.

West Jesmond House stood on the corner of Osborne
Road and Osborne Avenue alongside Burdon Place which
still exists. It was demolished around 1970 along with its
neighbour Tyneholme.The medical theme continued with
the opening of the Nuffield Hospital in 1973 on the site once
occupied by these two grand houses.

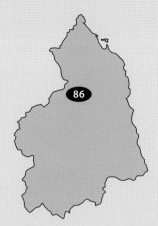

Whickhope Lodge

FALSTONE. *c.1850 - 1982 (under Kielder Water).*

Whickhope Lodge was built as a shooting box for the fourth Duke of Northumberland, circa 1850. The Duke owned vast tracts in the North Tyne Valley, much of which was tenanted as large sheep farms. They had to be large because the grazing was of a very poor quality. The name Whickhope has been given to an inlet of Keilder Water under which the remains of Whickhope Lodge are now consigned.

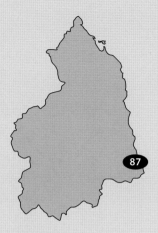

Whitley Hall

WHITLEY BAY. *c.1760. Wings added 1776 - 1899.*

Kelly's Post Office Directory of 1879 describes Whitley Bay as *"a popular and rising bathing place, with excellent sands"*. The four 'big houses' of the village are listed as Whitley Hall, Whitley House, Whitley Park and Whitley Villa – all now gone.

Whitley Hall was described as the residence of Mark William Lambert. It was built by the coal mine owning Hudson family, from who it descended to Hannah Ellison.

Hannah married John Carr, joining together two families – today represented by the Carr-Ellisons of Hedgeley Hall in Northumberland.

The site of the house, demolished in 1899, is now covered by Laburnham Avenue.

Whitley Park

WHITLEY BAY. *1789. Enlarged 1869 - 1939.*

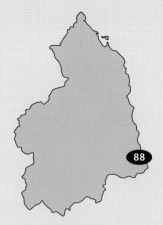

The original five bay Whitley Park of 1789 is shown to the left
of the view with the additions of 1869 shown to the right.
In 1897, the house became an hotel and its grounds covered
with housing. In 1922, it became Whitley Bay Council offices
which it remained until its demolition in 1939. Whitley Bay
Library now occupies its site.

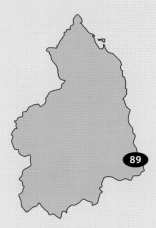

Whitley Villa (later Link House)

WHITLEY BAY.

89

Bulmer's Directory of 1887, shows Whitley Villa to be the home of the Greek Consul, Mr. Ernest Biesterfield. He could well be the gentleman shown above with his wife and parlour maid.

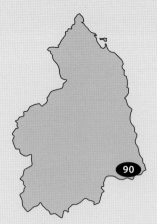

Willington House

WILLINGTON. *c.1800 - c.1950.*

90

90

Home in 1812 to colliery owner and viewer, John Watson.
As well as Willington Colliery, Watson also had those of
Collingwood main, Kenton, Fawdon and Denton under
his control. He was succeeded in his business interests as
well as at Willington House by his brother-in-law, George
Johnson and then by his nephew, John Johnson. The latter
married Miss Robson of West Chirton Hall, another lost
Northumberland mansion.

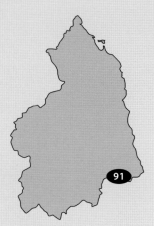

Wingrove House

ELSWICK. *c.1845 - 1903.*

91

Wingrove House was situated on Westgate Road and its site
is now occupied by Wingrove Road and its neighbouring
streets. Its grounds were adjacent to the estate of North
Elswick Hall which has itself recently been demolished.
Wingrove House was bought in 1866 by John Wigham
Richardson, a Shipbuilder, whose company amalgamated
with Swan Hunter in 1903. Cousins of the Richardson family
of Wheelbirks, the family left Wingrove and moved near to
their family to Hindley Hall near Stocksfield. Wingrove House
was demolished shortly after this.

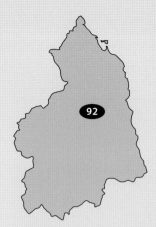

Woodside

HEPPLE. *c.1840s - c.1970.*

The Northumberland County History rather unkindly describes Woodside as:

"A comfortable stone house of no particular architectural distinction."

The house was built by the Riddell family in the 1840s and is very similar in style to the neighbouring Whitefield, which still survives. Woodside went circa 1970.

Saved for the future

Of course, it hasn't all been doom and gloom for Northumberland's country houses. Most still survive, and the outward signs of large estates, lodges, railings, parkland trees and distant glimpses of chimneys and towers can still be seen throughout the county.

Hesleyside has always been the home of the Charlton family, the Ridley's are still at Blagdon, the Swinburne's have been at Capheaton since it was built in 1668, and the recently built Swinburne Castle is home to Mrs. Richard Murphy, nee Mary Riddell. The Riddell's have lived at Swinburne since 1678, when they inherited the estate from their Widdrington ancestors.

The Mitford estate was in the Mitford family's ownership since before the Norman Conquest and was sold by them as recently as 1992. Many more country houses have found new, sympathetic owners and been restored to their former glory.

Swinburne Castle

Perhaps the most important and influential book to bring the fate of many of England's lost houses to a wider public view was the 'Destruction of the Country House', based on the 1974 Victoria and Albert Museum Exhibition. This listed only fifteen major losses in Northumberland but this pioneering work greatly underestimated the county's true losses.
It also included **Swinburne Castle**, shown left, which was demolished in 1964. It was survived by a sixteenth century wing and eighteenth century orangery and stable block. These have now been rejoined to the new Swinburne Castle completed in 2002. So much for those who thought that the age of the country house was over.

Examples of other ruinous houses which have been saved are **Kirkheaton Manor House** and **Lemmington Hall**.

Kirkheaton is a sixteenth century strong house re-fronted in the mid-seventeenth century. Added to this is a square Georgian addition of circa 1740 shown to the right of the view above. The house had become ruinous by 1920 as can be seen by the Collier postcard view (above). W.P. Collier of Bellingham took most of the early postcard views of the North Tyne and Coquet Valleys. His bicycle is often shown in his earlier views but by the time this view of Kirkheaton was taken, he had progressed to driving a motor bike. The house was restored circa 1930.

Lemmington Hall near Edlingham was another house which could easily have been lost. A fifteenth century tower house

with an eighteenth century country house added to it had become the roofless shell shown on page 102, circa 1905.

It was restored in 1913 by Sir Stephen Aitchison, whose family have only recently left the Red House in Stocksfield and is shown below in pristine condition.

Lemmington Hall

Fallodon Hall

Fallodon Hall of circa 1730 burnt down in 1917. Sir Edward Grey lived in the kitchen wing while the main block was remodelled and rebuilt between 1921-1924.

The picture above shows the house before the fire. The view after rebuilding (below) shows that the second floor was not reinstated.

Fire was named as one of the earliest reasons for houses being lost. **Fenham Hall** (left) was burnt out in 1908. An important house with a south front of 1748 by Daniel Garrett, and a north front of circa 1800 by William Newton, it was restored shortly after the fire.

Fenham Hall

Fallodon Hall

Kirkley Hall near Ponteland was also a victim of fire in 1928. The original house of 1764 was replaced in 1832 by the house designed by Ignatius Bonomi shown below.

Kirkley Hall, before the fire.

This was replaced after the fire by the present Kirkley Hall, designed by R. Burns Dick. The second floor was not re-built.

Kirkley Hall, rebuilt.

Pallinsburn, before reduction.

Several country house owners did not wait for fire to reduce their houses by removing the second floor. Work started on eighteenth century **Pallinsburn** in 1912, but the job was closed down in August 1914 on account of the start of the First World War. It wasn't until 1933 that Charles Mitchell finally removed the top storey and replaced it with a flat concrete roof. The three pictures shown here are a dramatic record of the original house, work in progress, and the present reduced Pallinsburn.

Work in progress at Pallinsburn.

Pallinsburn, after reduction.

Bythorne in Corbridge was also reduced in size in the 1920s. Originally called The Willows, Bythorne (below) was enlarged and re-named in the 1870s. The 1920s alterations saw the clock tower and second floor removed to save on energy and staff costs.

Early eighteenth century **Roddam Hall** lost its second floor in 1979 as part of a major restoration of the house by Lord Vinson. The two storey present Roddam Hall has lost the typical Northumbrian bleakness so evident in this view (below) of the house before alteration.

Bythorne, Corbridge.

Roddam Hall

*Blenkinsopp Hall, shown left,
and below after reduction c.1950.*

Eshott Hall

Not all houses were made smaller by removal of the top storey. Eighteenth Century **Blenkinsopp Hall** near Haltwhistle had large additions in 1835 by Dobson, and was further extended in 1877. The two views of the house (above) clearly show how drastically the house was reduced circa 1950. Removal of Dobson's tower to the right of the view together with the attached three bays of the main house make it much more manageable. It is still home to the Joicey family.

Eshott Hall, probably built by Robert Trollope in 1660, has had a curious history. The original house, shown to the left of this picture, was extended in the 1820s by the five bay block shown in the centre. The house was further extended in 1881 by the addition of the three bay wing to the right, copying the style of the original house. In the 1950s the central block was demolished forming two separate houses. This lost block was replaced in 1999 with the architectural detail taken from a postcard view, (possibly the one shown left) of the original house.

Benwell Tower

Northumberland's Lost Houses

The houses indicated in **bold type** are number referenced to the Gazetteer (on pages 11 to103).

Anderson Place - Grey St., Newcastle. 1

Bank House - Acklington. 2

Bath House - Bath Lane, Newcastle

Beacon Grange - Hexham. 3

Beaconsfield House - Cullercoats. 4

Bebside Hall - Bedlington

Bedlington Old Hall - Bedlington. 5

Beech Grove - Elswick, Newcastle

Bellshill - Adderstone. 6

Benton Grange - Benton

Benton Hall - Benton. 7

Benton Lodge - Benton

Benton Park - Benton. 8

Benwell Cottage - Benwell, Newcastle. 9

Benwell Grange - Benwell, Newcastle

Benwell Grove - Benwell, Newcastle. 10

Benwell Hall - Benwell, Newcastle. 11

Benwell House - Benwell, Newcastle. 12

Benwell Lodge - Benwell, Newcastle

Benwell Old House - Benwell, Newcastle

Benwell Park - Benwell, Newcastle

Bewshaugh - Keilder. 13

Biddlestone Hall - Alwinton. 14

Birdhope Craig - Rochester. 15

Birtley Hall - Wark

Black Hedley (Gatehouse). 16

Blenkinsopp Castle - Blenkinsopp. 17

Bonny Rigg Hall - Bardon Mill. 18

Bothal Haugh - Bothal. 19

Brandon White House - Ingram

Broom Park - Bolton. 20

Broomfield Tower - Jesmond, Newcastle (later The Minories)

Bygate Hall - Alwinton. 21

Byker Hall - Byker, Newcastle

Bykerhill House - Byker, Newcastle

Byker House - Byker, Newcastle

Campville - North Shields

Carville Hall - Wallsend. 22

Castle Hill Pele - Haltwhistle. 23

The Chase - Cowpen. 24

Chirton Hall - Chirton

Chirton House - Chirton. 25

Cleveland House - North Shields

Collingwood House - Whittingham (formerly Unthank Hall)

Condercum House - Benwell, Newcastle. 26

Condercum Villa - Benwell, Newcastle

Cowpen Grove - Cowpen. 27

Cowpen Hall - Cowpen. 28

Cowpen House - Cowpen. 29

Coxlodge Hall - Gosforth, Newcastle. 30

Cramlington House - Cramlington

Cresswell Hall - Cresswell. 31

Cross House - Spital Tongues, Newcastle. 32

Cross House - Westgate Road, Newcastle

Crow Hall - Cramlington

Seaton Lodge.

Newburn Hall

Acknowledgements

The majority of the images featured in this book are taken from Jim Davidson's vast collection of historic postcards. In addition, we are grateful to the following people for giving permission to use their photographs:

West Newcastle Picture History Collection:
9, 11, 12, 36, 58 & 63.

Mr. Andrew Bridges: 18 & 85.

North Tyneside Library: 25.

Dr. Thomas Faulkner: 39.

Newcastle Libraries, Local Studies: 62.

Hilary Kristensen: 69 & 71.

National Monuments Record: 80.

Text and images © Jim Davidson 2008.

Designed and produced by Iain Kerr Associates
01434 634895. www.iainkerrassociates.co.uk

Printed by Elanders Hindson, Newcastle upon Tyne.

First published in December 2008 by
Wagtail Press,
Gairshield, Steel,
Hexham, Northumberland,
NE47 0HS.

www.wagtailpress.co.uk

WAGTAIL PRESS

ISBN: 978 - 0 - 9538443 - 9 - 5